GRAPHIC LIBRARY

DISASTERS IN HISTORY

THE 1918 FLU PANDEMIC

by Katherine Krohn

illustrated by Bob Hall, Keith Williams,
and Charles Barnett III

Consultant:

John M. Barry, author
*The Great Influenza: The Epic Story
of the Deadliest Plague in History*

Capstone *press*

Mankato, Minnesota

Graphic Library is published by Capstone Press,
151 Good Counsel Drive, P.O. Box 669, Mankato, Minnesota 56002.
www.capstonepress.com

Printed in the United States of America

1 2 3 4 5 6 12 11 10 09 08 07

Library of Congress Cataloging-in-Publication Data
Krohn, Katherine E.
The 1918 flu pandemic / by Katherine Krohn; illustrated by Bob Hall, Keith Williams, and Charles Barnett, III.
p. cm.—(Graphic library. Disasters in history)
Summary: "In graphic novel format, follows the 1918 outbreak of a mysterious influenza virus that killed millions of people worldwide, making it the deadliest pandemic in history"—Provided by publisher.
Includes bibliographical references and index.
ISBN-13: 978-1-4296-0158-0 (hardcover)
ISBN-10: 1-4296-0158-2 (hardcover)
1. Influenza—History—Juvenile literature. I. Hall, Bob. II. Williams, Keith. III. Barnett, Charles, III. IV. Title. V. Series.
RC150.4.K76 2008
614.5'180904—dc22 2007000004

Designers
Thomas Emery and Ted Williams

Colorist
Brent Schoonover

Editor
Christine Peterson

Editor's note: Direct quotations from primary sources are indicated by a yellow background.

Direct quotations appear on the following page:
Page 12, from *A Doctor's Memories* by Victor C. Vaughan (Indianapolis: The Bobbs-Merrill Company, 1926).

TABLE OF CONTENTS

Chapter 1
An Invisible Threat

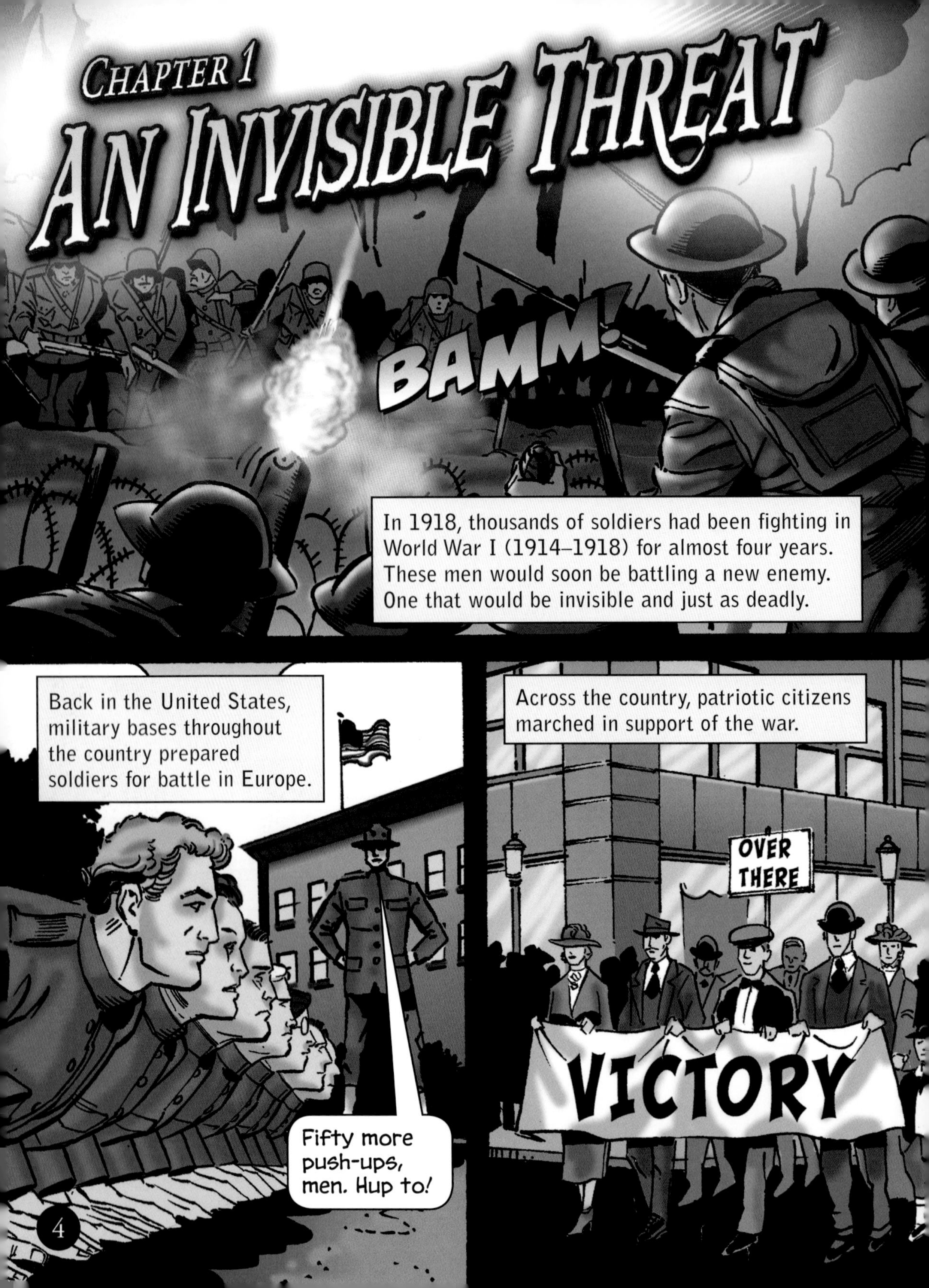
BAMM!
In 1918, thousands of soldiers had been fighting in World War I (1914–1918) for almost four years. These men would soon be battling a new enemy. One that would be invisible and just as deadly.
Back in the United States, military bases throughout the country prepared soldiers for battle in Europe.
Fifty more push-ups, men. Hup to!
Across the country, patriotic citizens marched in support of the war.
OVER THERE
VICTORY

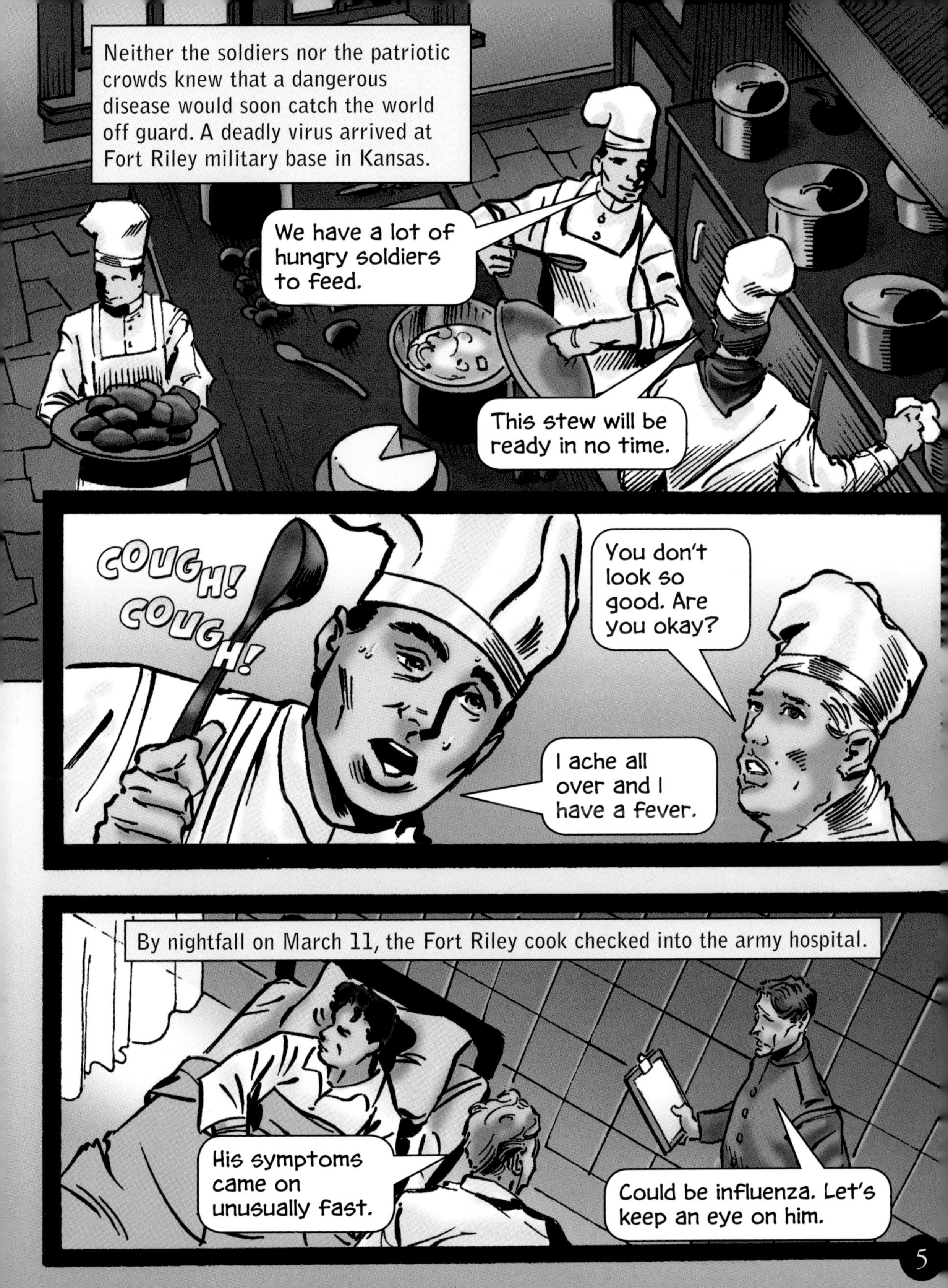
Neither the soldiers nor the patriotic crowds knew that a dangerous disease would soon catch the world off guard. A deadly virus arrived at Fort Riley military base in Kansas.
We have a lot of hungry soldiers to feed.
This stew will be ready in no time.
COUGH! COUGH!
You don't look so good. Are you okay?
I ache all over and I have a fever.
By nightfall on March 11, the Fort Riley cook checked into the army hospital.
His symptoms came on unusually fast.
Could be influenza. Let's keep an eye on him.

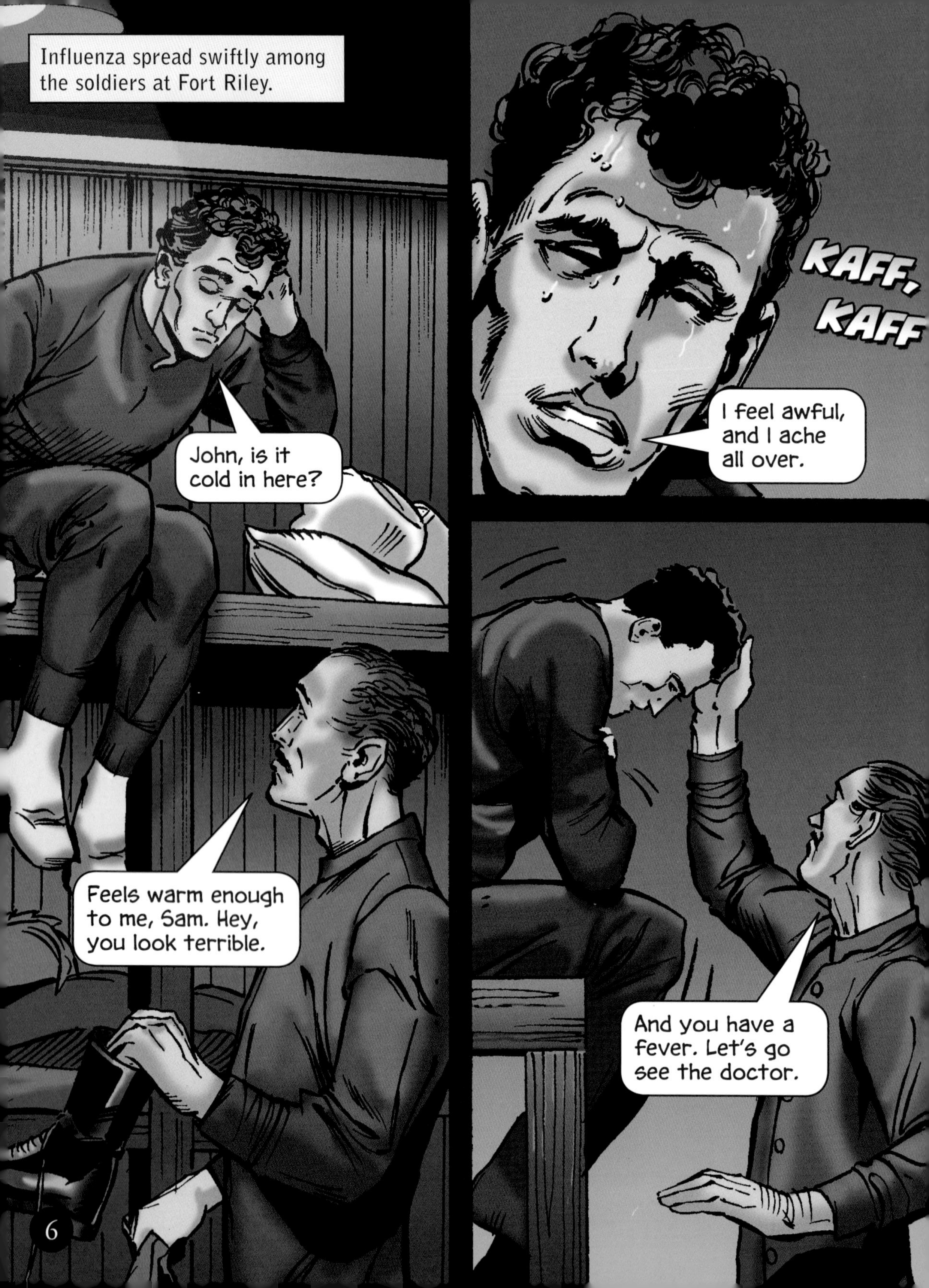
Influenza spread swiftly among the soldiers at Fort Riley.
John, is it cold in here?
Feels warm enough to me, Sam. Hey, you look terrible.
KAFF, KAFF
I feel awful, and I ache all over.
And you have a fever. Let's go see the doctor.

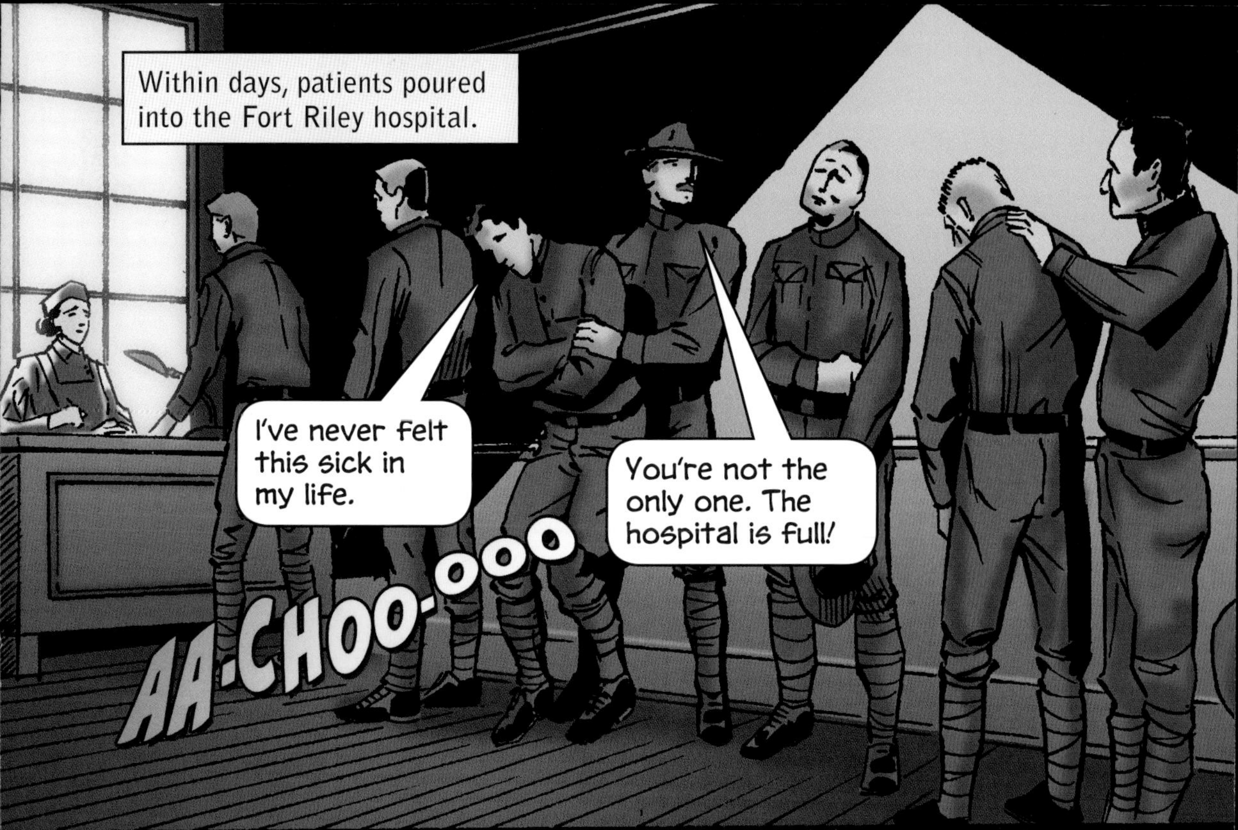
Within days, patients poured into the Fort Riley hospital.
I've never felt this sick in my life.
You're not the only one. The hospital is full!
AA-CHOO-OOO

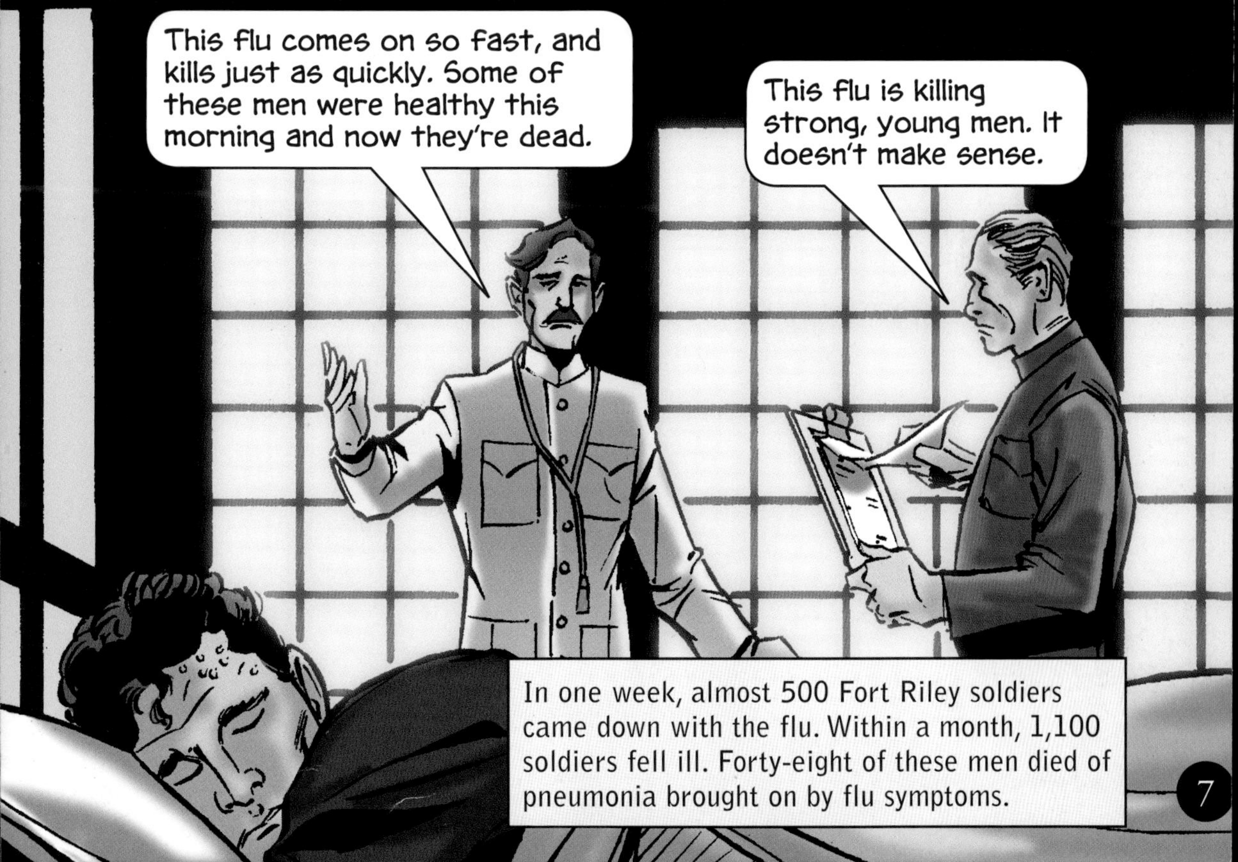
This flu comes on so fast, and kills just as quickly. Some of these men were healthy this morning and now they're dead.
This flu is killing strong, young men. It doesn't make sense.
In one week, almost 500 Fort Riley soldiers came down with the flu. Within a month, 1,100 soldiers fell ill. Forty-eight of these men died of pneumonia brought on by flu symptoms.

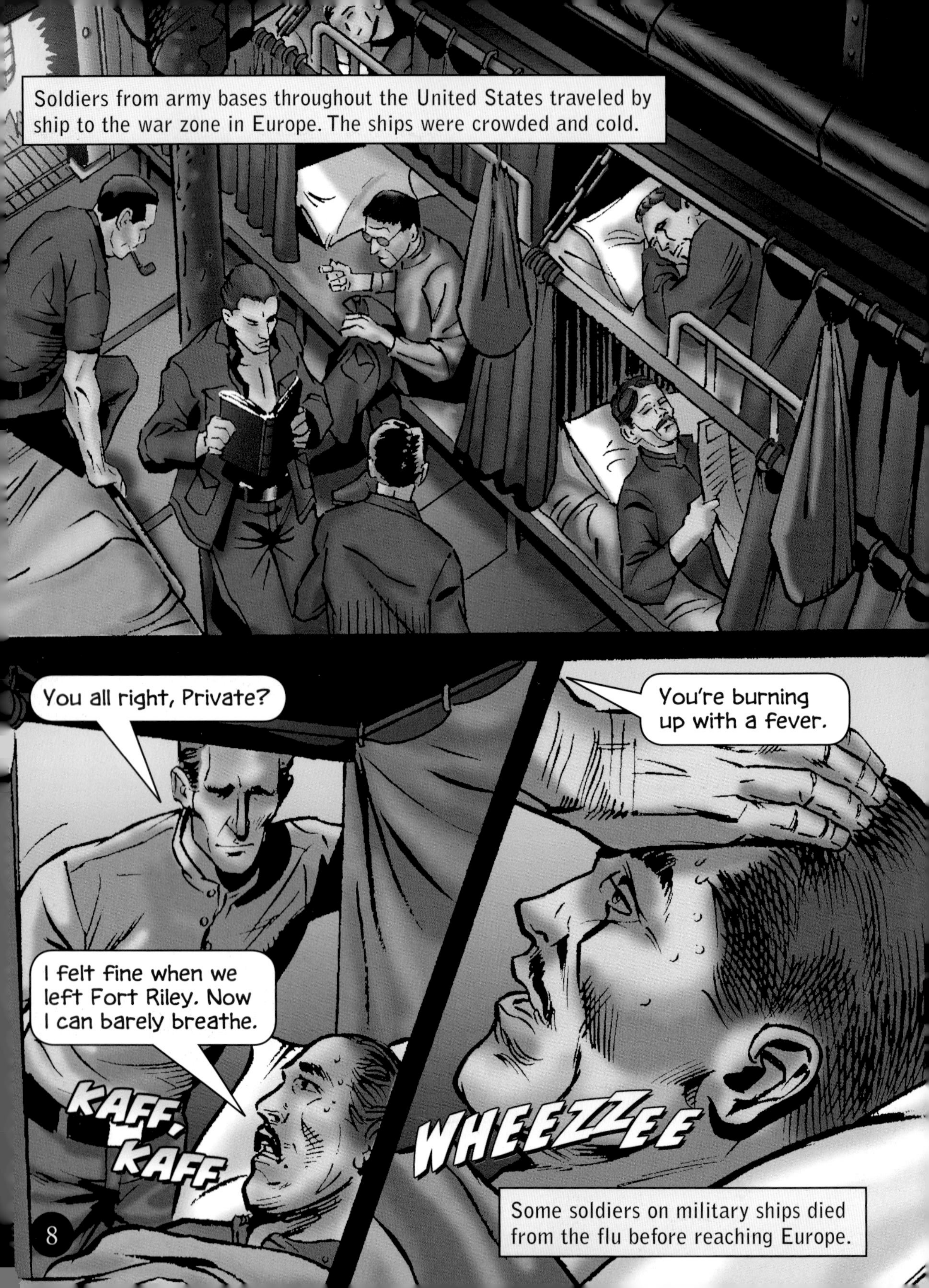
Soldiers from army bases throughout the United States traveled by ship to the war zone in Europe. The ships were crowded and cold.
You all right, Private?
I felt fine when we left Fort Riley. Now I can barely breathe.
KAFF, KAFF
You're burning up with a fever.
WHEEZZEE
Some soldiers on military ships died from the flu before reaching Europe.

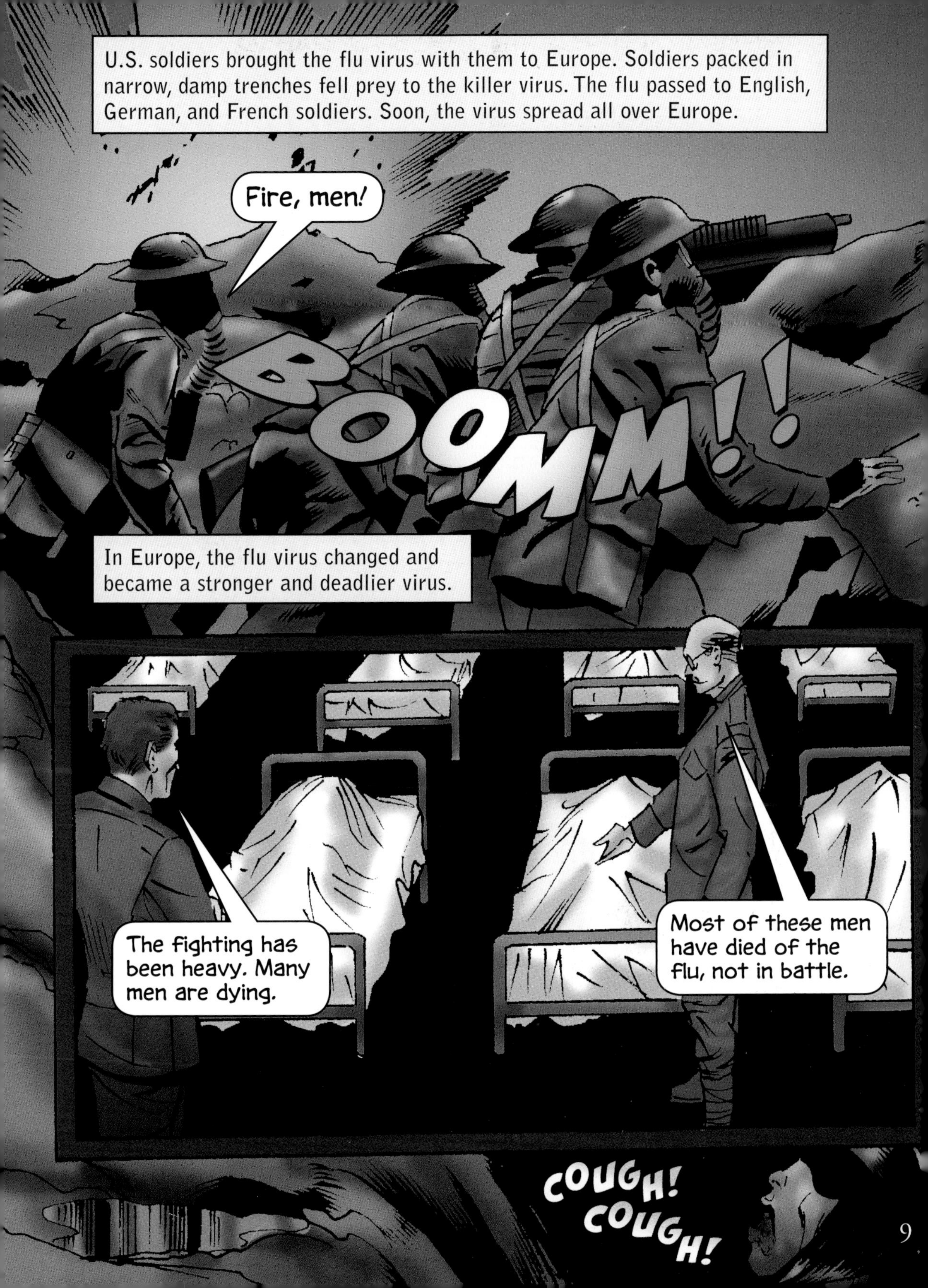
U.S. soldiers brought the flu virus with them to Europe. Soldiers packed in narrow, damp trenches fell prey to the killer virus. The flu passed to English, German, and French soldiers. Soon, the virus spread all over Europe.
Fire, men!
BOOMM!!
In Europe, the flu virus changed and became a stronger and deadlier virus.
The fighting has been heavy. Many men are dying.
Most of these men have died of the flu, not in battle.
COUGH! COUGH!

Chapter 2
The Danger Spreads

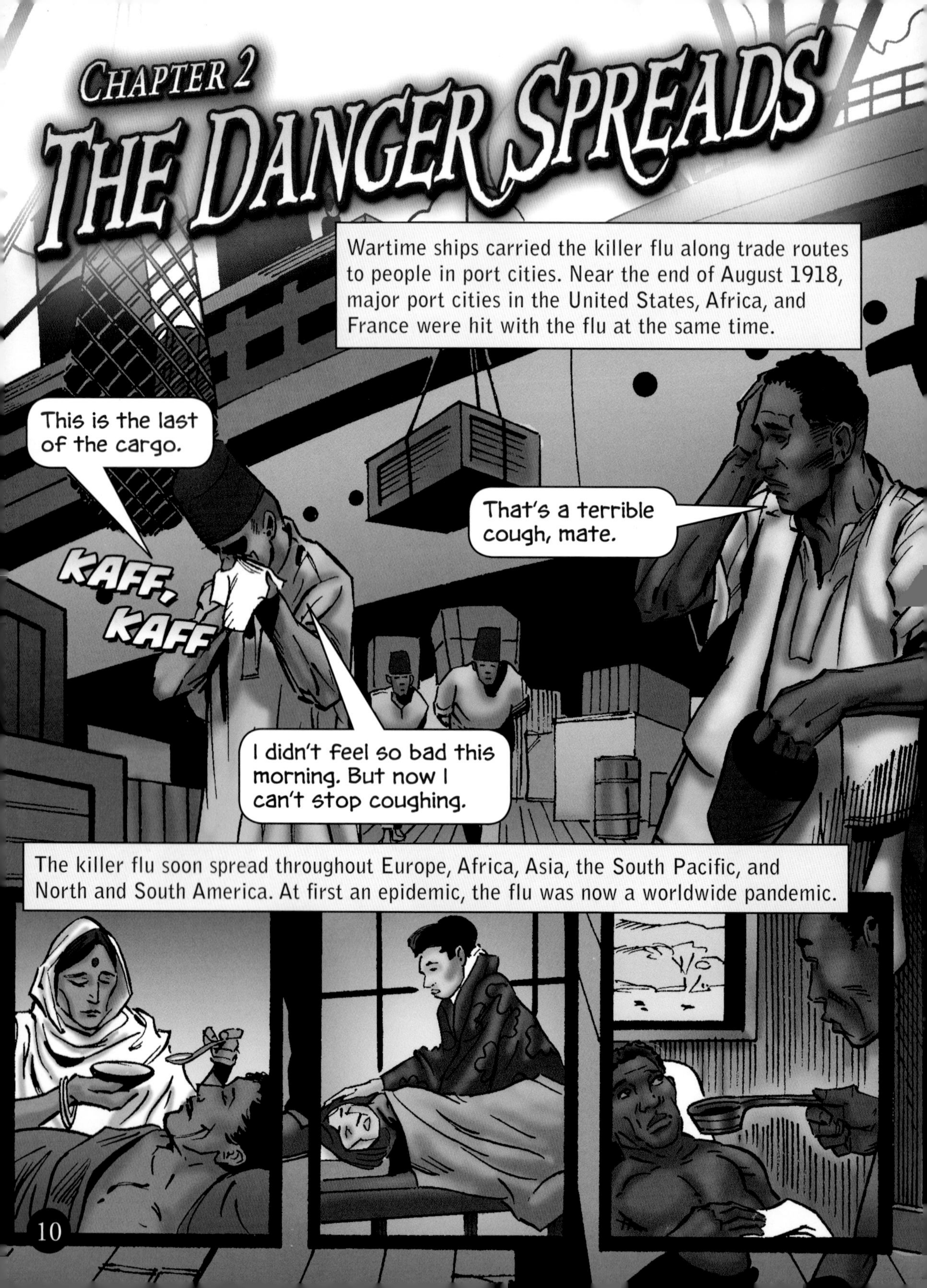
Wartime ships carried the killer flu along trade routes to people in port cities. Near the end of August 1918, major port cities in the United States, Africa, and France were hit with the flu at the same time.
This is the last of the cargo.
KAFF, KAFF
That's a terrible cough, mate.
I didn't feel so bad this morning. But now I can't stop coughing.
The killer flu soon spread throughout Europe, Africa, Asia, the South Pacific, and North and South America. At first an epidemic, the flu was now a worldwide pandemic.

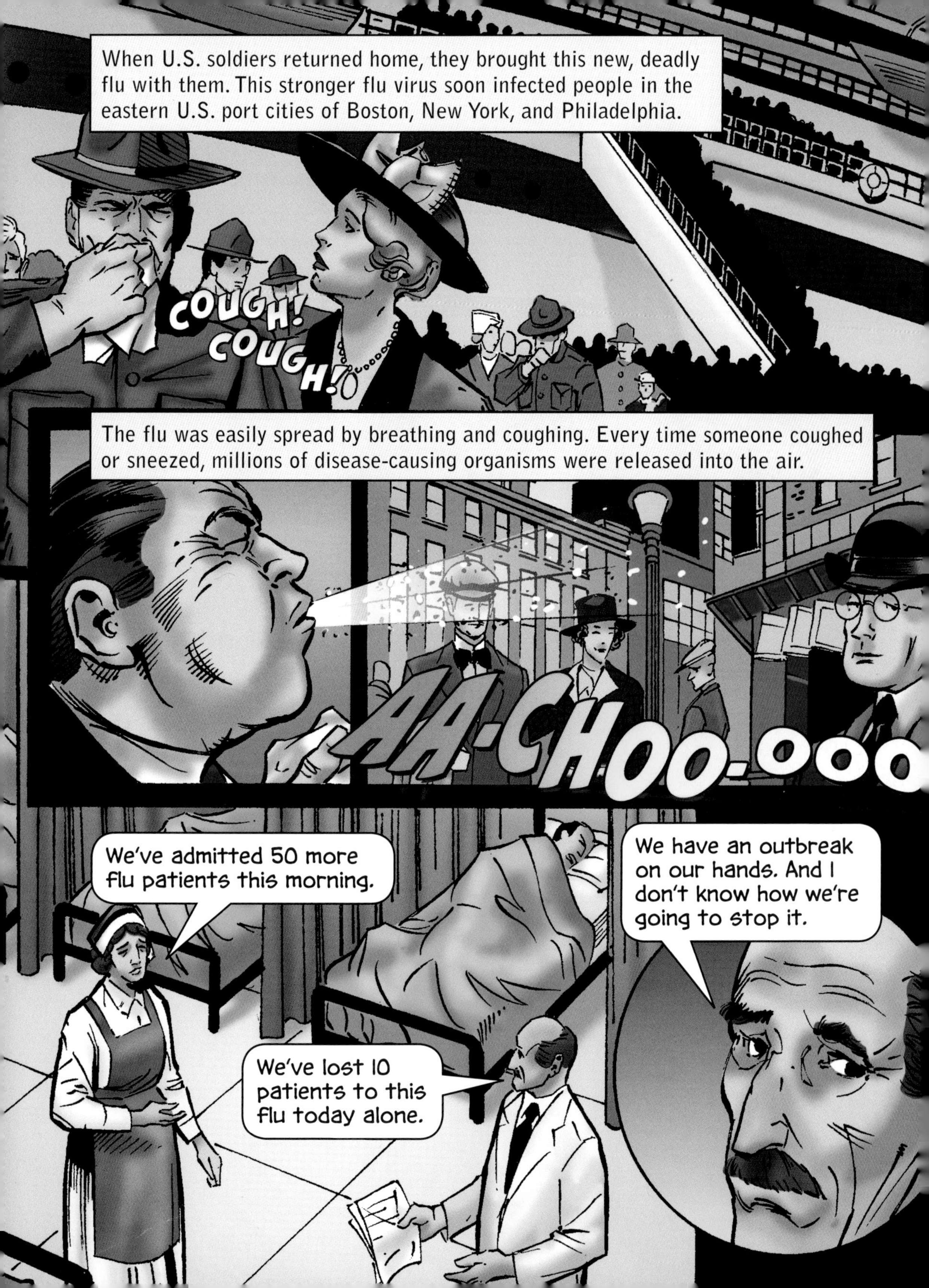
When U.S. soldiers returned home, they brought this new, deadly flu with them. This stronger flu virus soon infected people in the eastern U.S. port cities of Boston, New York, and Philadelphia.
COUGH! COUGH!
The flu was easily spread by breathing and coughing. Every time someone coughed or sneezed, millions of disease-causing organisms were released into the air.
AA-CHOO-OOO
We've admitted 50 more flu patients this morning.
We've lost 10 patients to this flu today alone.
We have an outbreak on our hands. And I don't know how we're going to stop it.

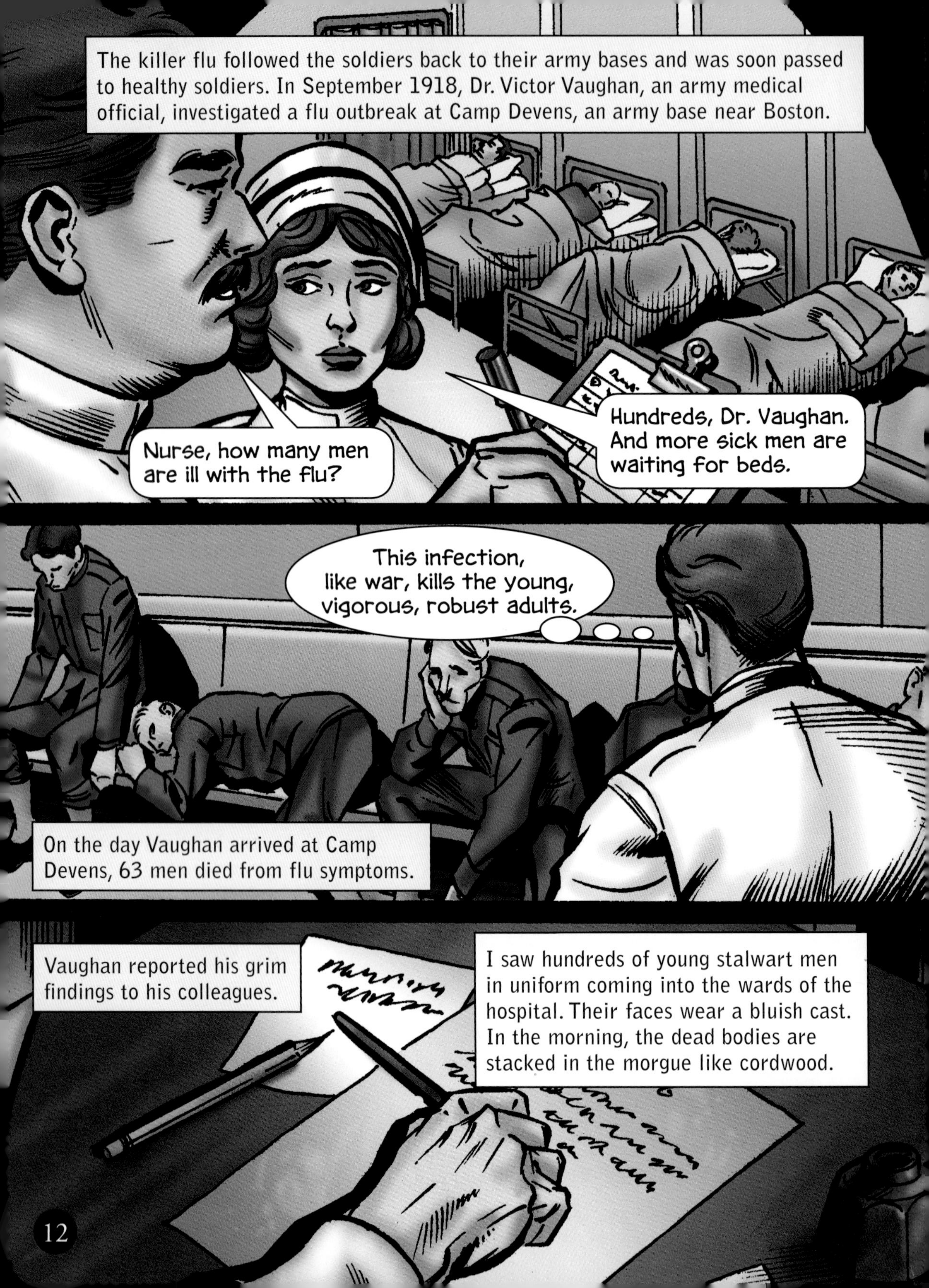
The killer flu followed the soldiers back to their army bases and was soon passed to healthy soldiers. In September 1918, Dr. Victor Vaughan, an army medical official, investigated a flu outbreak at Camp Devens, an army base near Boston.
Nurse, how many men are ill with the flu?
Hundreds, Dr. Vaughan. And more sick men are waiting for beds.
This infection, like war, kills the young, vigorous, robust adults.
On the day Vaughan arrived at Camp Devens, 63 men died from flu symptoms.
Vaughan reported his grim findings to his colleagues.
I saw hundreds of young stalwart men in uniform coming into the wards of the hospital. Their faces wear a bluish cast. In the morning, the dead bodies are stacked in the morgue like cordwood.

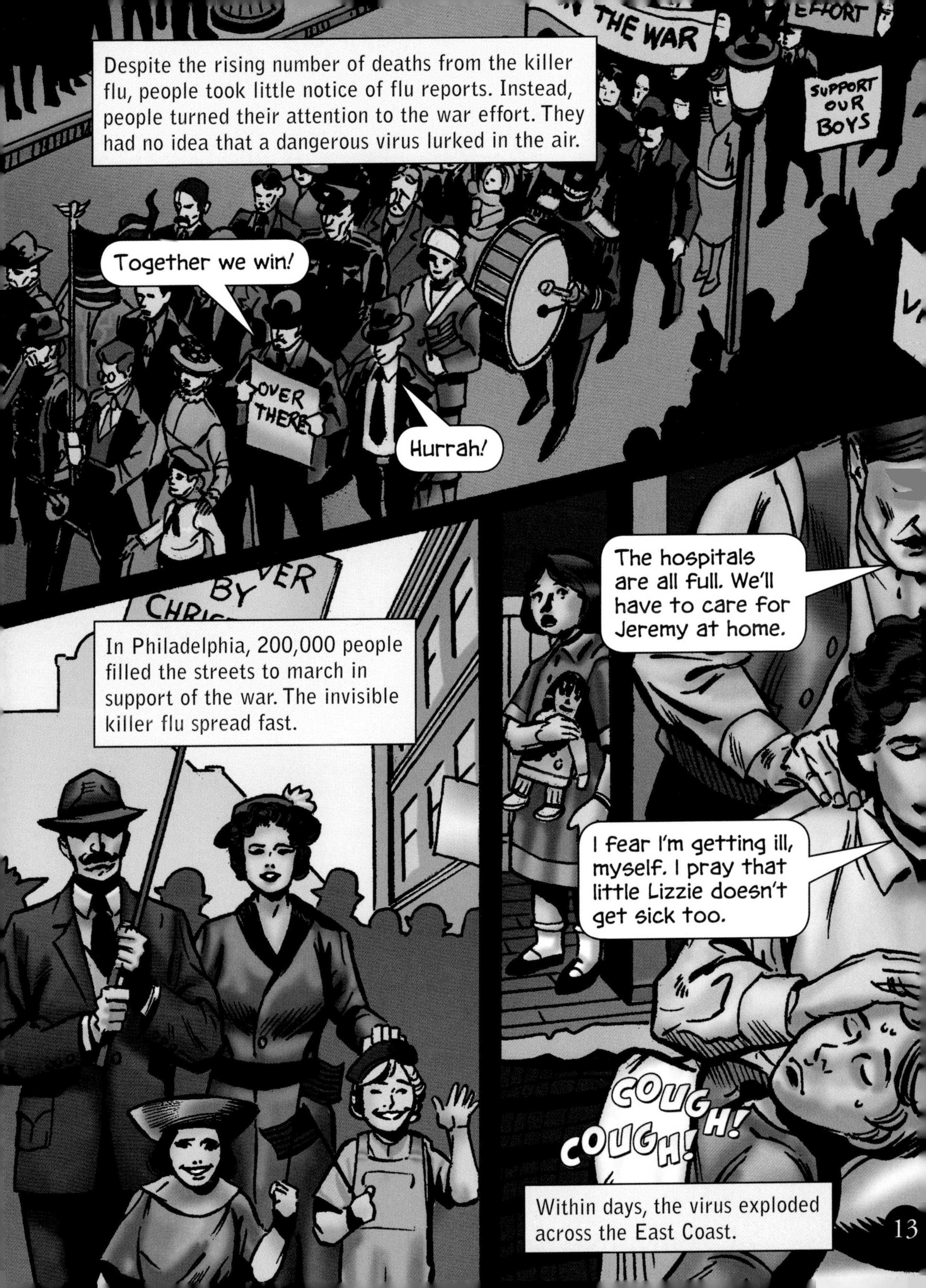
THE WAR
SUPPORT OUR BOYS
Despite the rising number of deaths from the killer flu, people took little notice of flu reports. Instead, people turned their attention to the war effort. They had no idea that a dangerous virus lurked in the air.
Together we win!
OVER THERE
Hurrah!
In Philadelphia, 200,000 people filled the streets to march in support of the war. The invisible killer flu spread fast.
The hospitals are all full. We'll have to care for Jeremy at home.
I fear I'm getting ill, myself. I pray that little Lizzie doesn't get sick too.
COUGH!
COUGH!
Within days, the virus exploded across the East Coast.

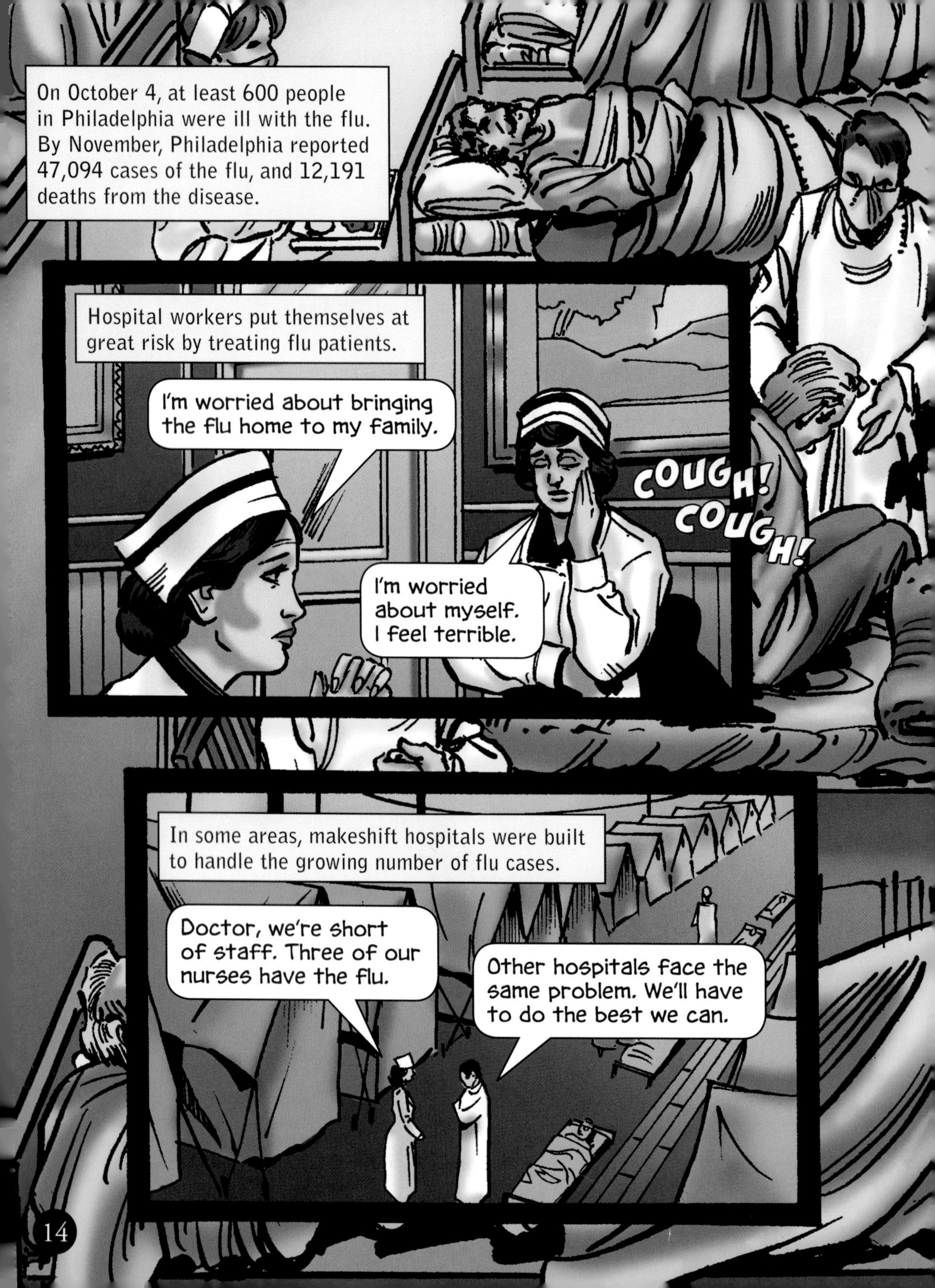
On October 4, at least 600 people in Philadelphia were ill with the flu. By November, Philadelphia reported 47,094 cases of the flu, and 12,191 deaths from the disease.
Hospital workers put themselves at great risk by treating flu patients.
I'm worried about bringing the flu home to my family.
I'm worried about myself. I feel terrible.
COUGH! COUGH!
In some areas, makeshift hospitals were built to handle the growing number of flu cases.
Doctor, we're short of staff. Three of our nurses have the flu.
Other hospitals face the same problem. We'll have to do the best we can.

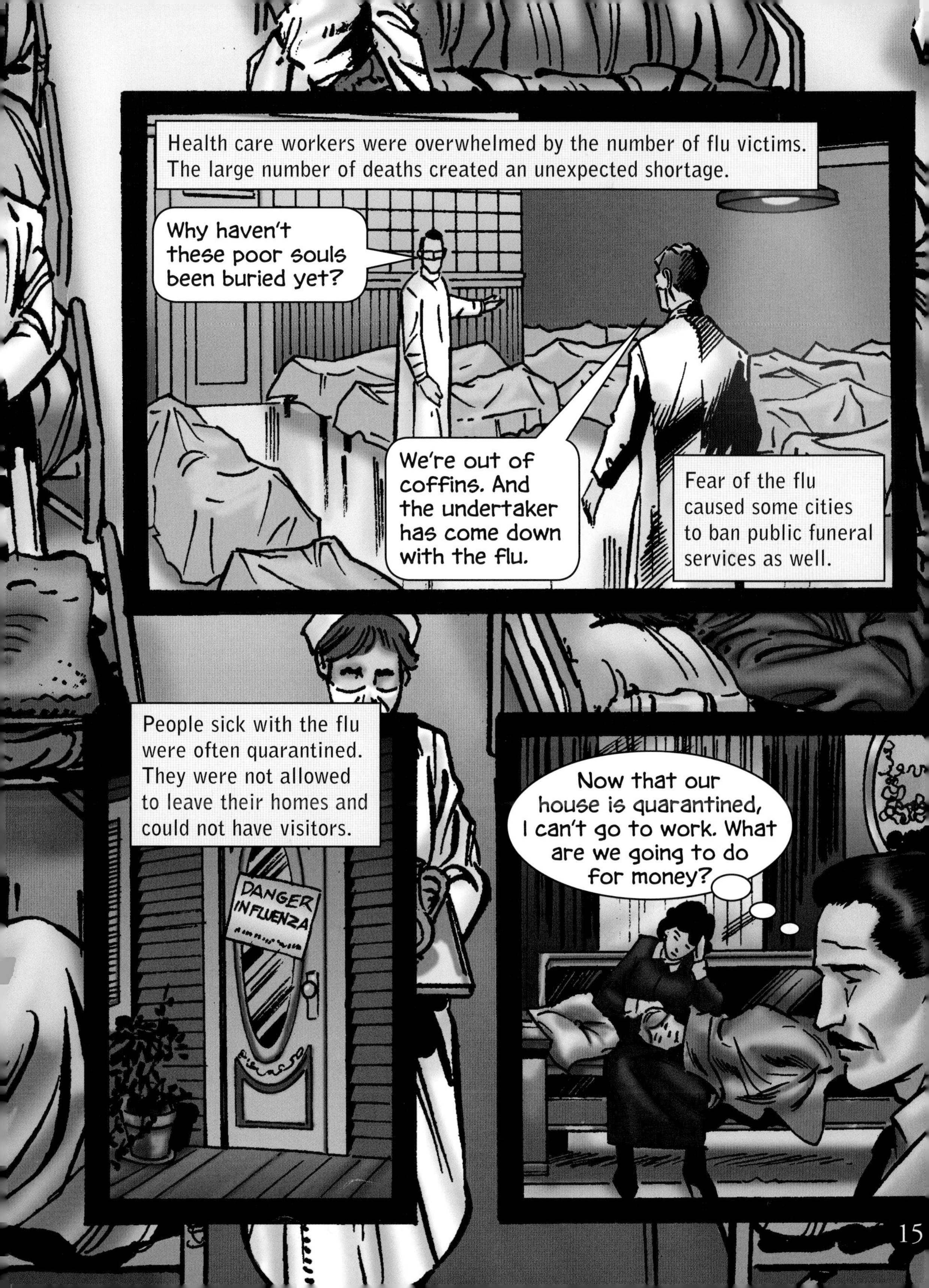
Health care workers were overwhelmed by the number of flu victims. The large number of deaths created an unexpected shortage.
Why haven't these poor souls been buried yet?
We're out of coffins. And the undertaker has come down with the flu.
Fear of the flu caused some cities to ban public funeral services as well.
People sick with the flu were often quarantined. They were not allowed to leave their homes and could not have visitors.
DANGER INFLUENZA
Now that our house is quarantined, I can't go to work. What are we going to do for money?

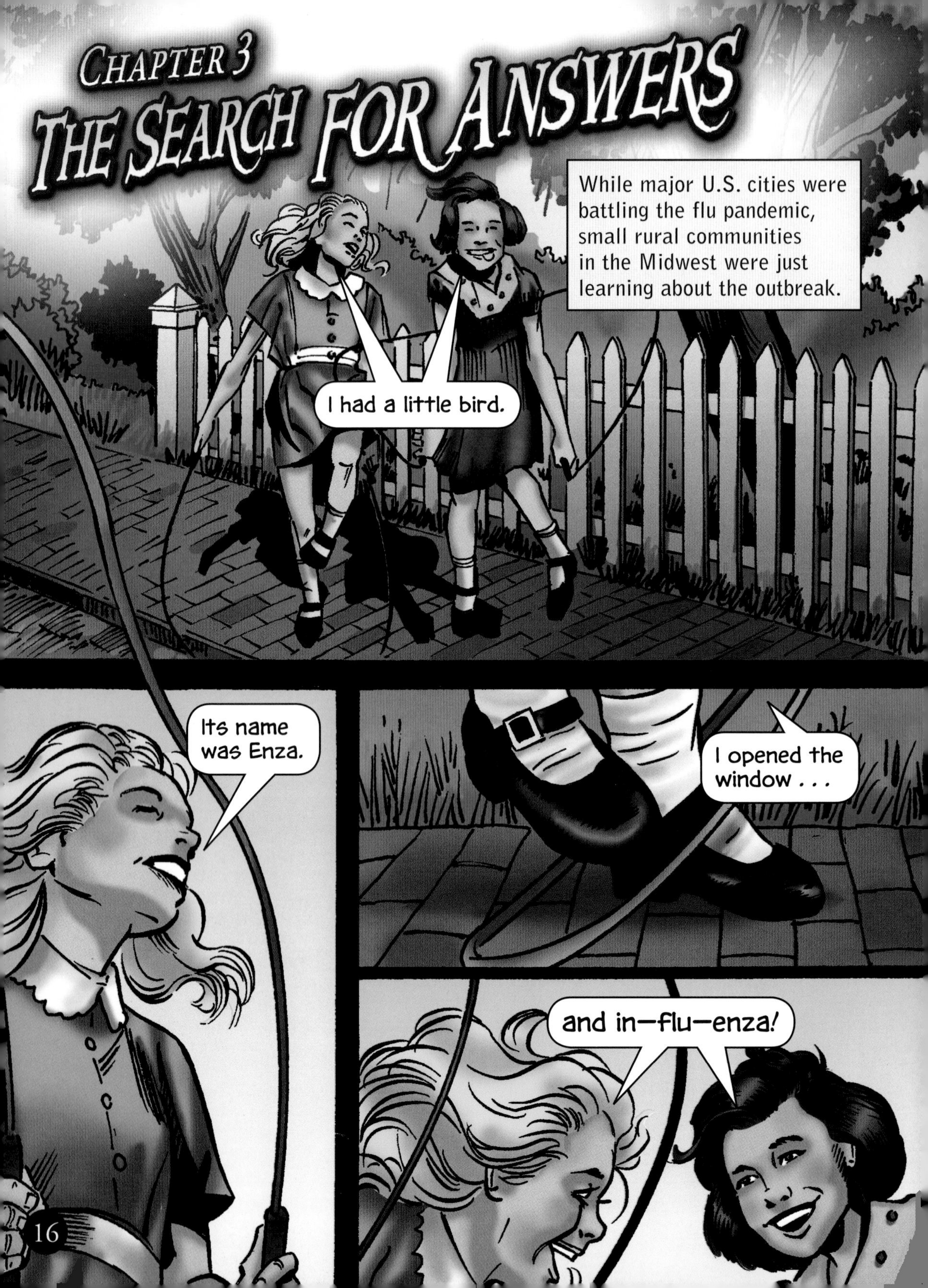
CHAPTER 3
THE SEARCH FOR ANSWERS
While major U.S. cities were battling the flu pandemic, small rural communities in the Midwest were just learning about the outbreak.
I had a little bird.
Its name was Enza.
I opened the window . . .
and in—flu—enza!

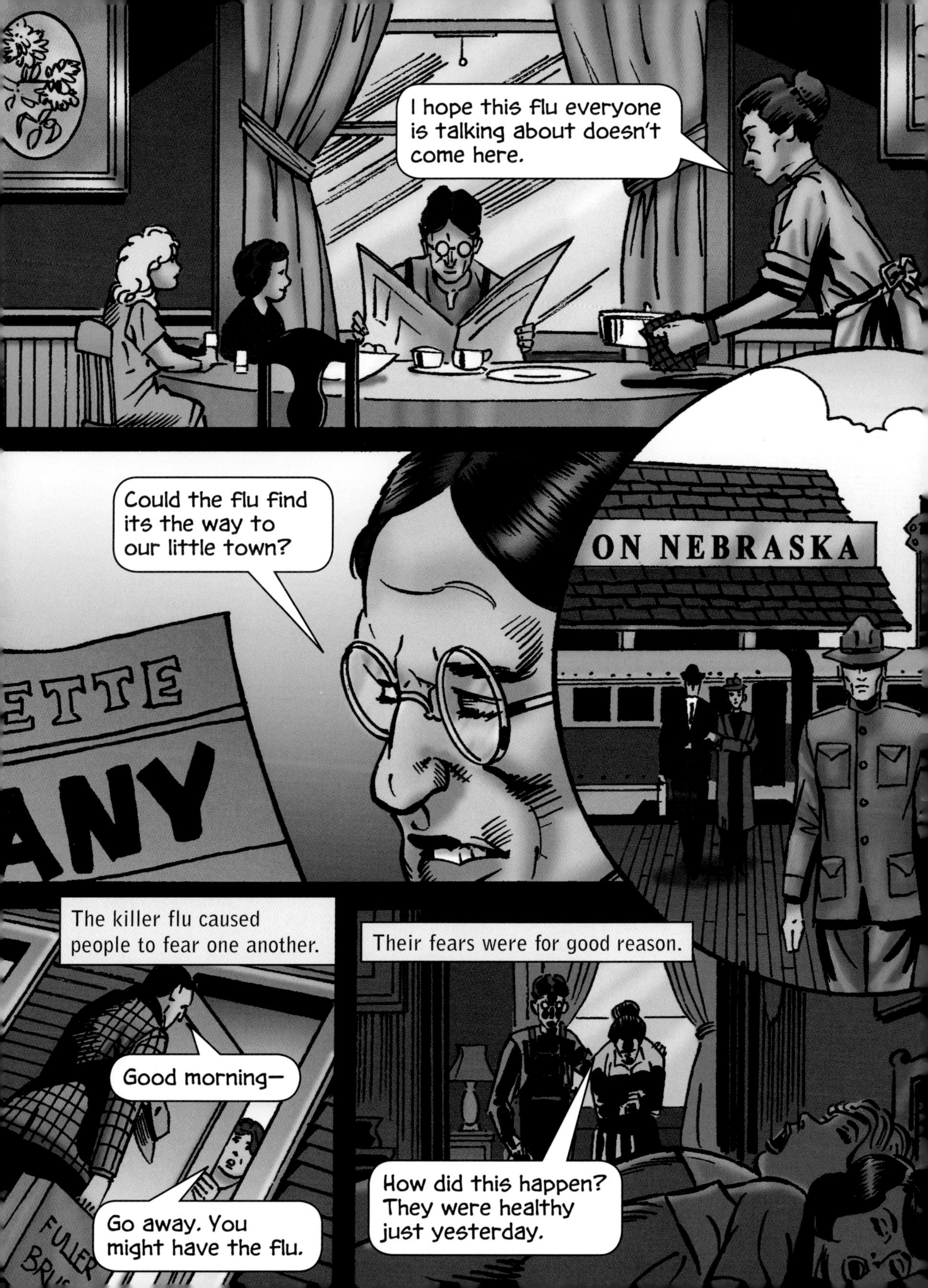
I hope this flu everyone is talking about doesn't come here.
Could the flu find its the way to our little town?
ETTE
ANY
ON NEBRASKA
The killer flu caused people to fear one another.
Good morning—
Go away. You might have the flu.
FULLER
Their fears were for good reason.
How did this happen? They were healthy just yesterday.

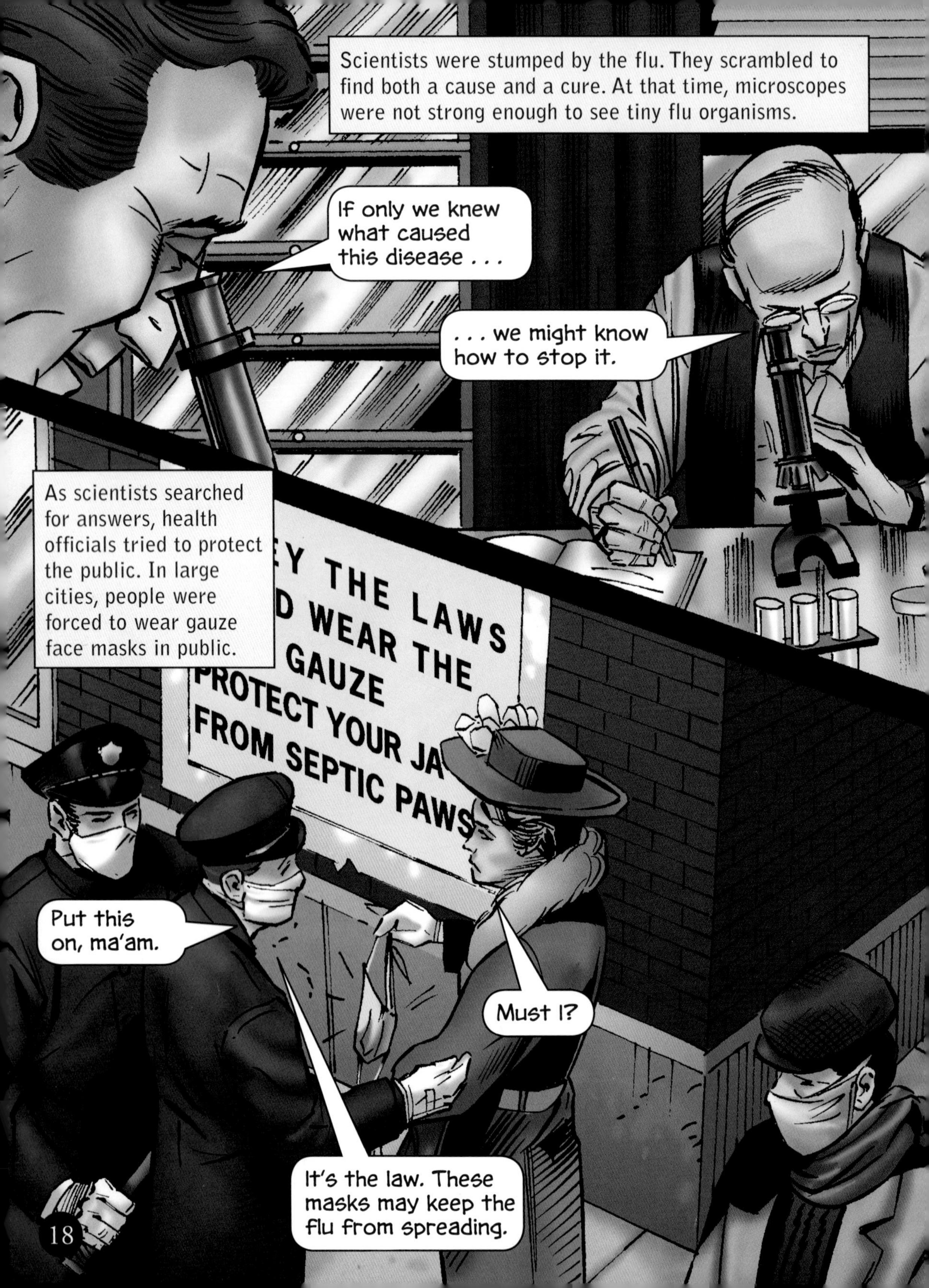

Scientists were stumped by the flu. They scrambled to find both a cause and a cure. At that time, microscopes were not strong enough to see tiny flu organisms.
If only we knew what caused this disease . . .
. . . we might know how to stop it.
As scientists searched for answers, health officials tried to protect the public. In large cities, people were forced to wear gauze face masks in public.
EY THE LAWS
D WEAR THE
GAUZE
PROTECT YOUR JA
FROM SEPTIC PAWS
Put this on, ma'am.
Must I?
It's the law. These masks may keep the flu from spreading.

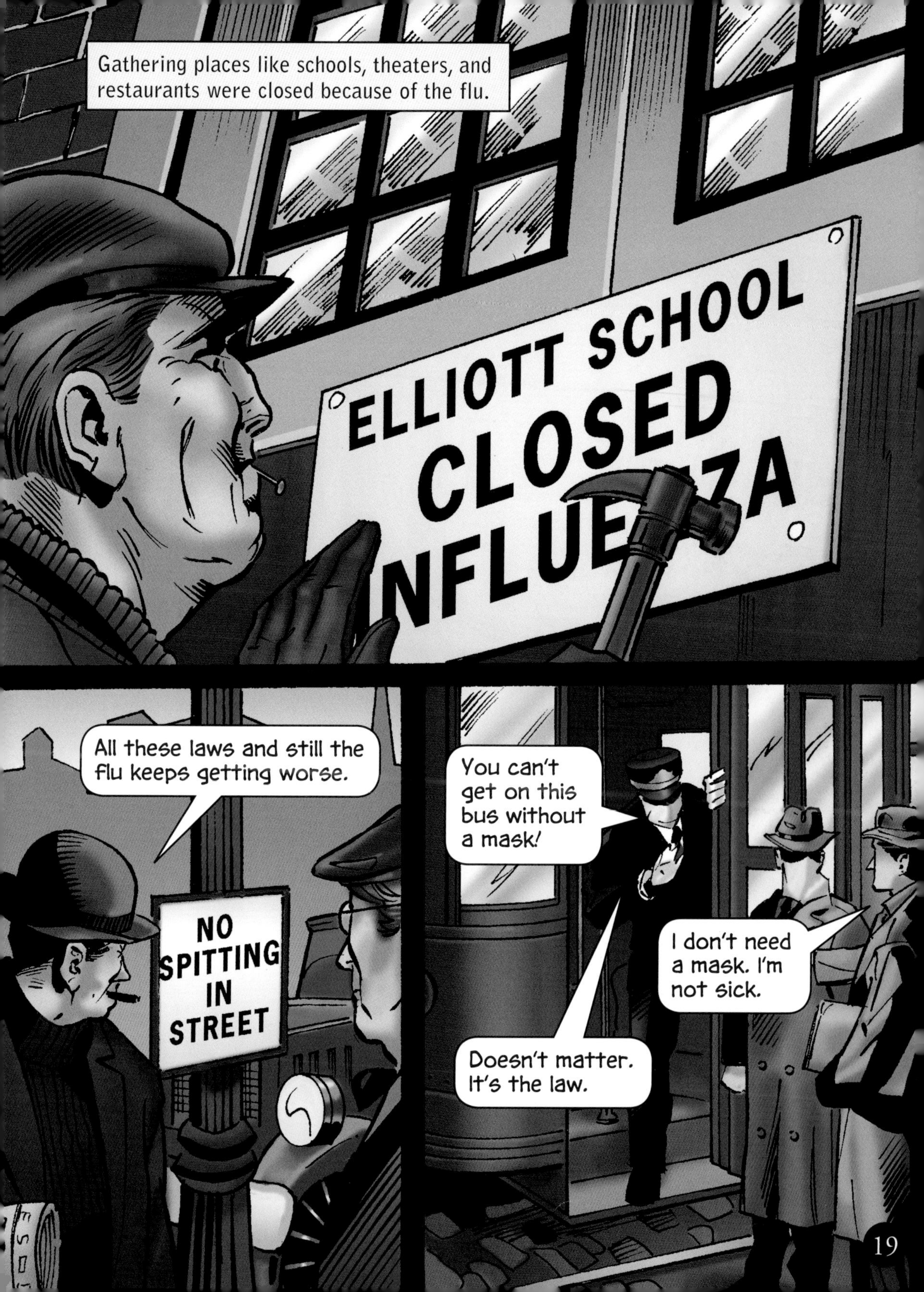
Gathering places like schools, theaters, and restaurants were closed because of the flu.
ELLIOTT SCHOOL
CLOSED
INFLUE ZA
All these laws and still the flu keeps getting worse.
NO SPITTING IN STREET
You can't get on this bus without a mask!
I don't need a mask. I'm not sick.
Doesn't matter. It's the law.

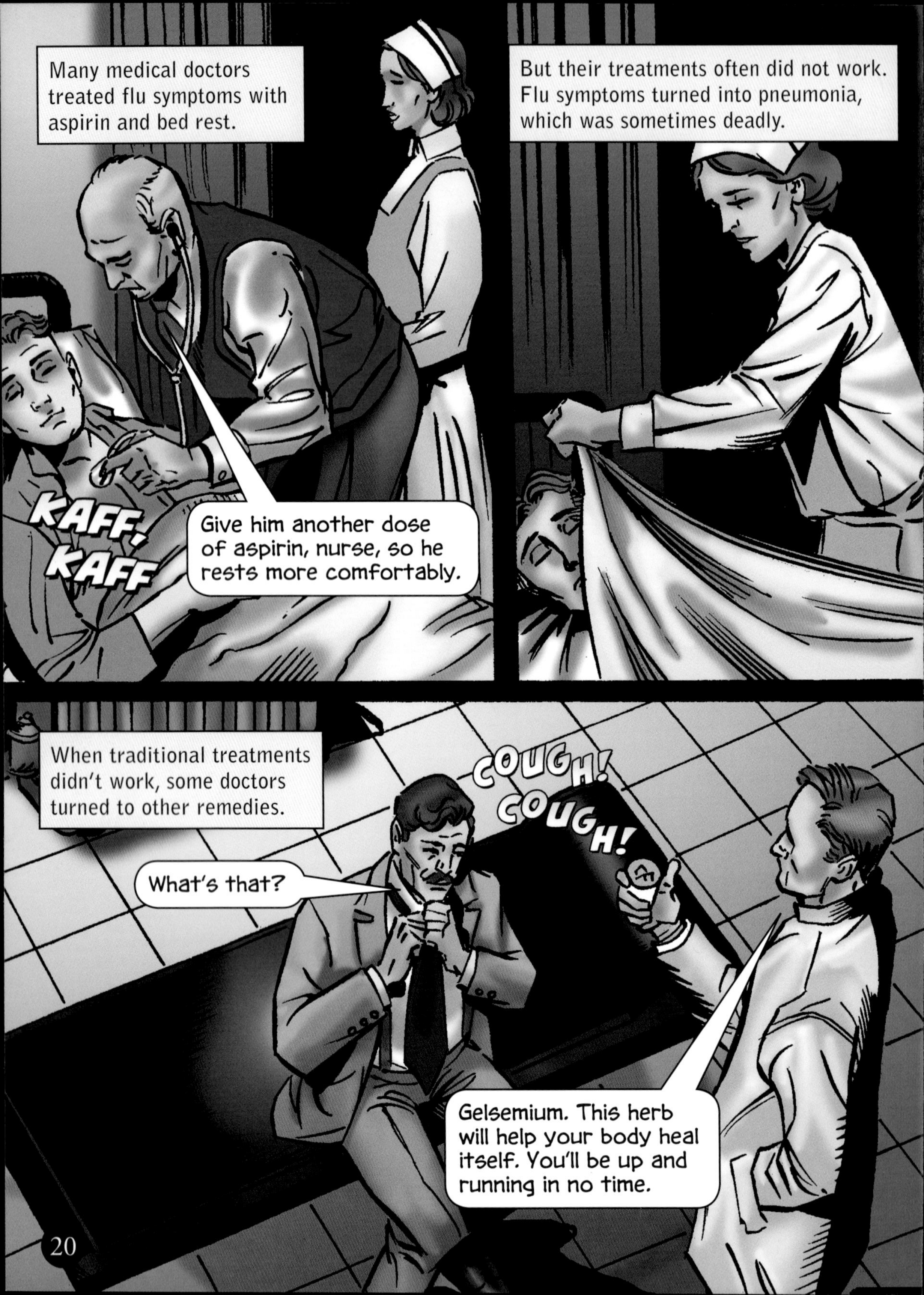
Many medical doctors treated flu symptoms with aspirin and bed rest.
KAFF, KAFF
Give him another dose of aspirin, nurse, so he rests more comfortably.
But their treatments often did not work. Flu symptoms turned into pneumonia, which was sometimes deadly.
When traditional treatments didn't work, some doctors turned to other remedies.
COUGH! COUGH!
What's that?
Gelsemium. This herb will help your body heal itself. You'll be up and running in no time.

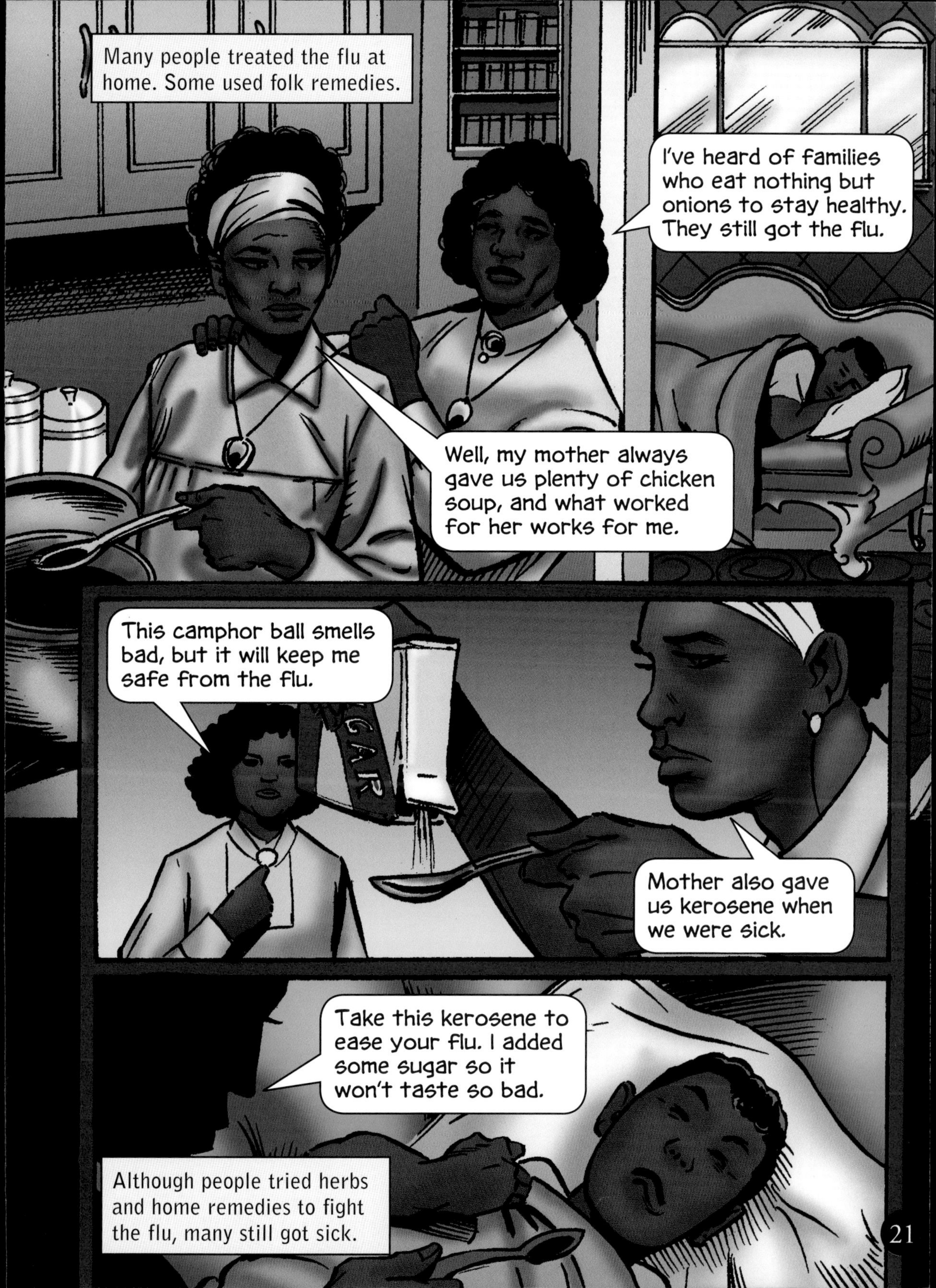

Many people treated the flu at home. Some used folk remedies.
I've heard of families who eat nothing but onions to stay healthy. They still got the flu.
Well, my mother always gave us plenty of chicken soup, and what worked for her works for me.
This camphor ball smells bad, but it will keep me safe from the flu.
GAR
Mother also gave us kerosene when we were sick.
Take this kerosene to ease your flu. I added some sugar so it won't taste so bad.
Although people tried herbs and home remedies to fight the flu, many still got sick.

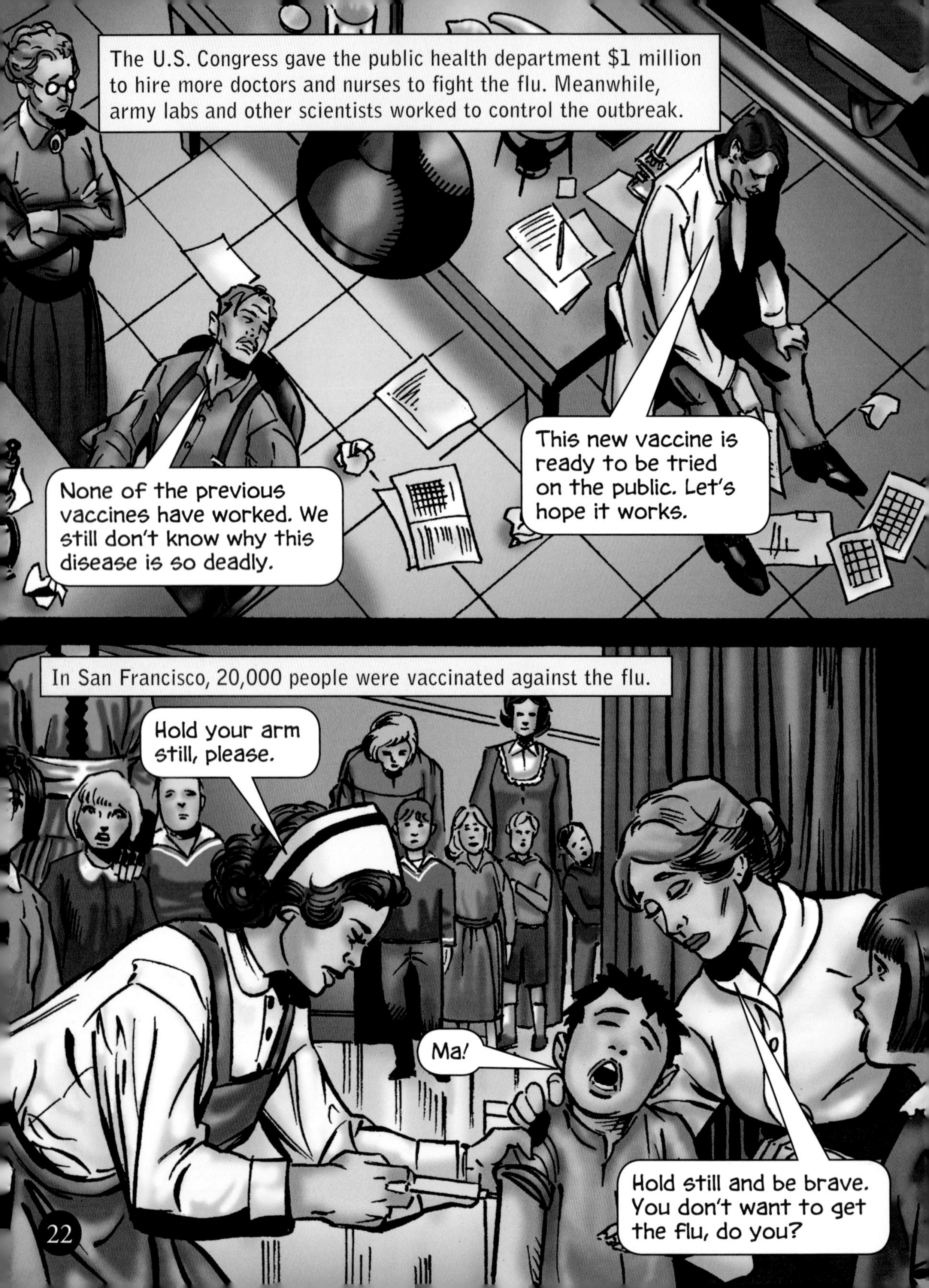
The U.S. Congress gave the public health department $1 million to hire more doctors and nurses to fight the flu. Meanwhile, army labs and other scientists worked to control the outbreak.
None of the previous vaccines have worked. We still don't know why this disease is so deadly.
This new vaccine is ready to be tried on the public. Let's hope it works.
In San Francisco, 20,000 people were vaccinated against the flu.
Hold your arm still, please.
Ma!
Hold still and be brave. You don't want to get the flu, do you?

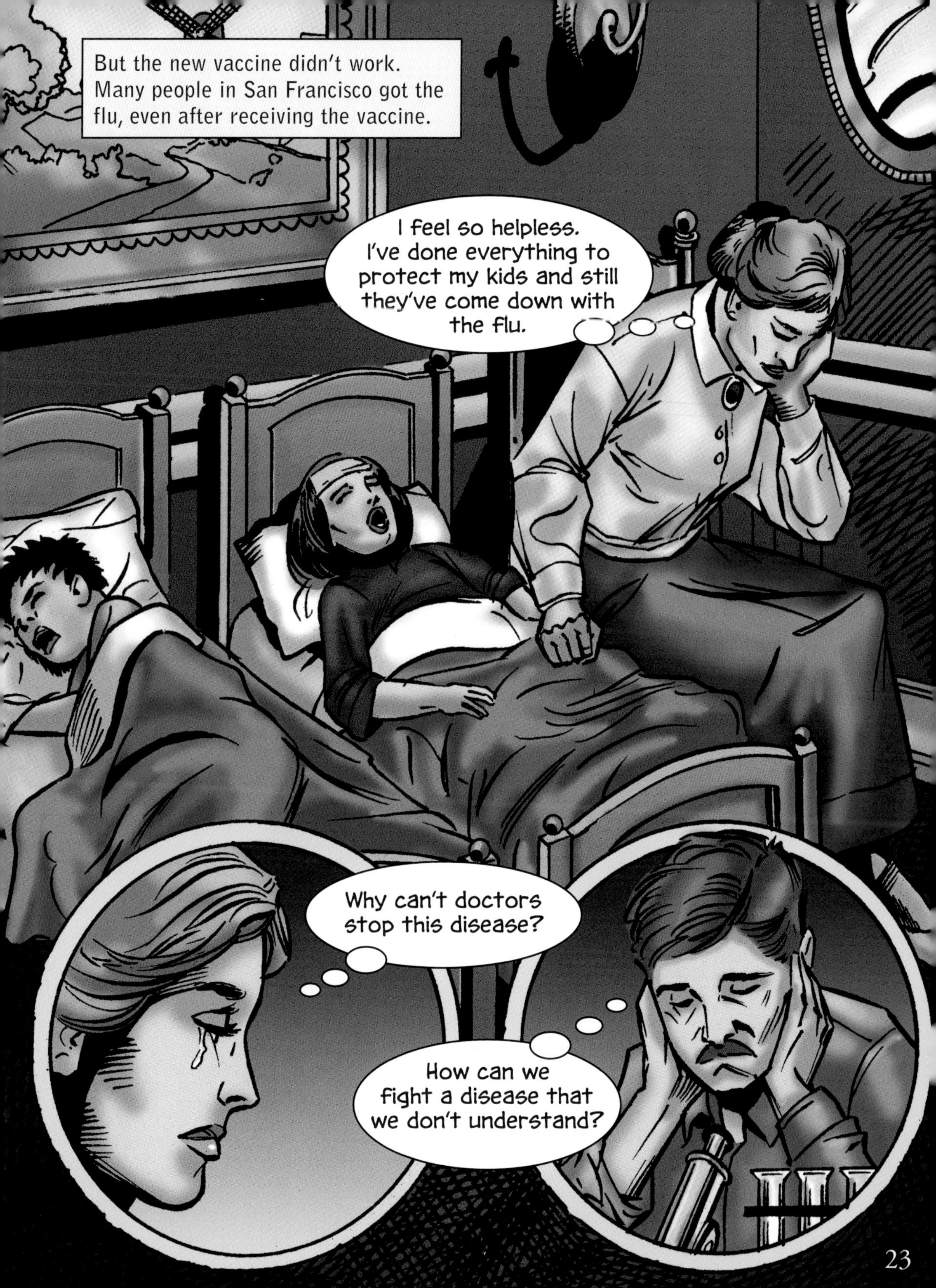
But the new vaccine didn't work. Many people in San Francisco got the flu, even after receiving the vaccine.
I feel so helpless. I've done everything to protect my kids and still they've come down with the flu.
Why can't doctors stop this disease?
How can we fight a disease that we don't understand?

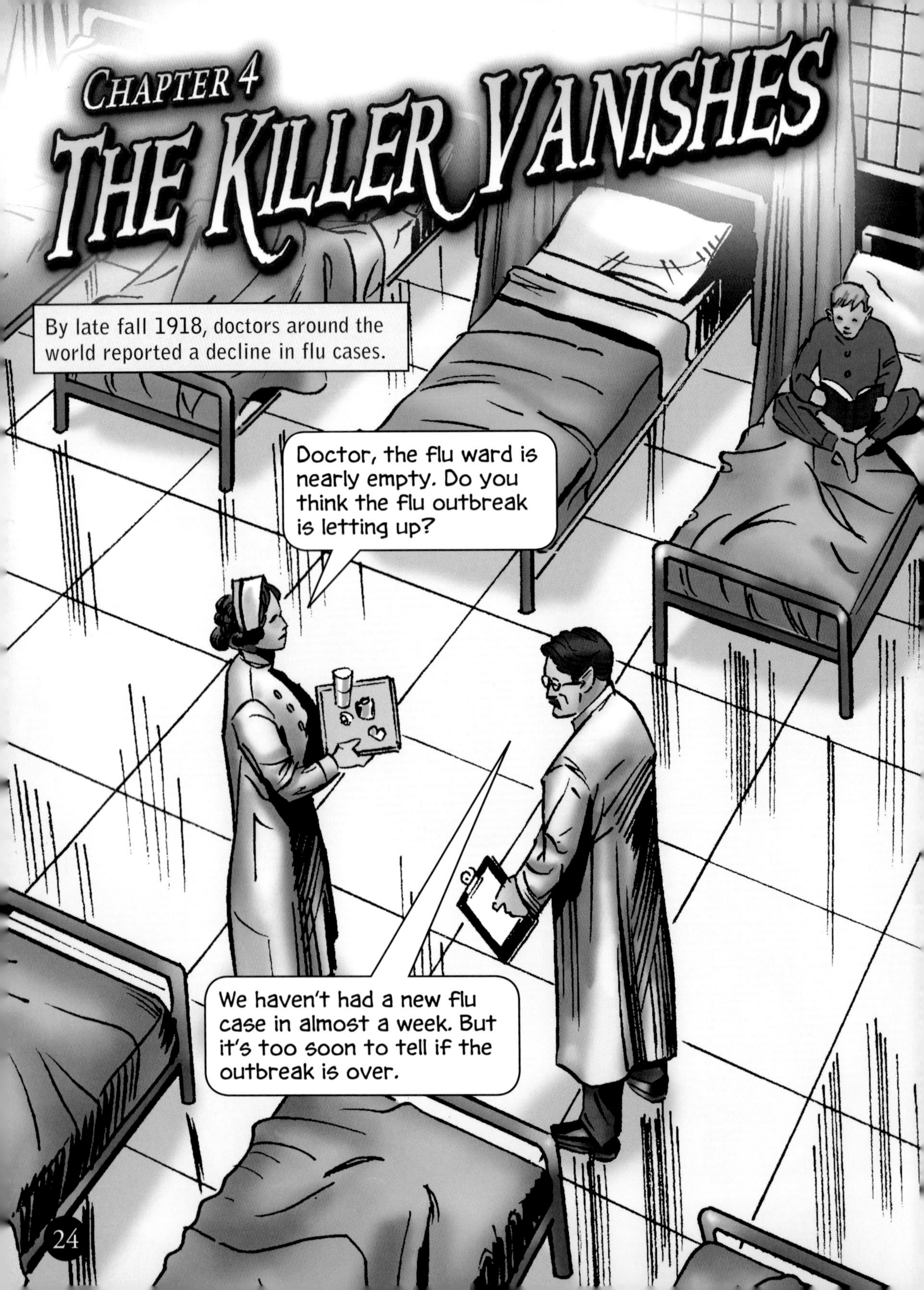
CHAPTER 4
THE KILLER VANISHES
By late fall 1918, doctors around the world reported a decline in flu cases.
Doctor, the flu ward is nearly empty. Do you think the flu outbreak is letting up?
We haven't had a new flu case in almost a week. But it's too soon to tell if the outbreak is over.

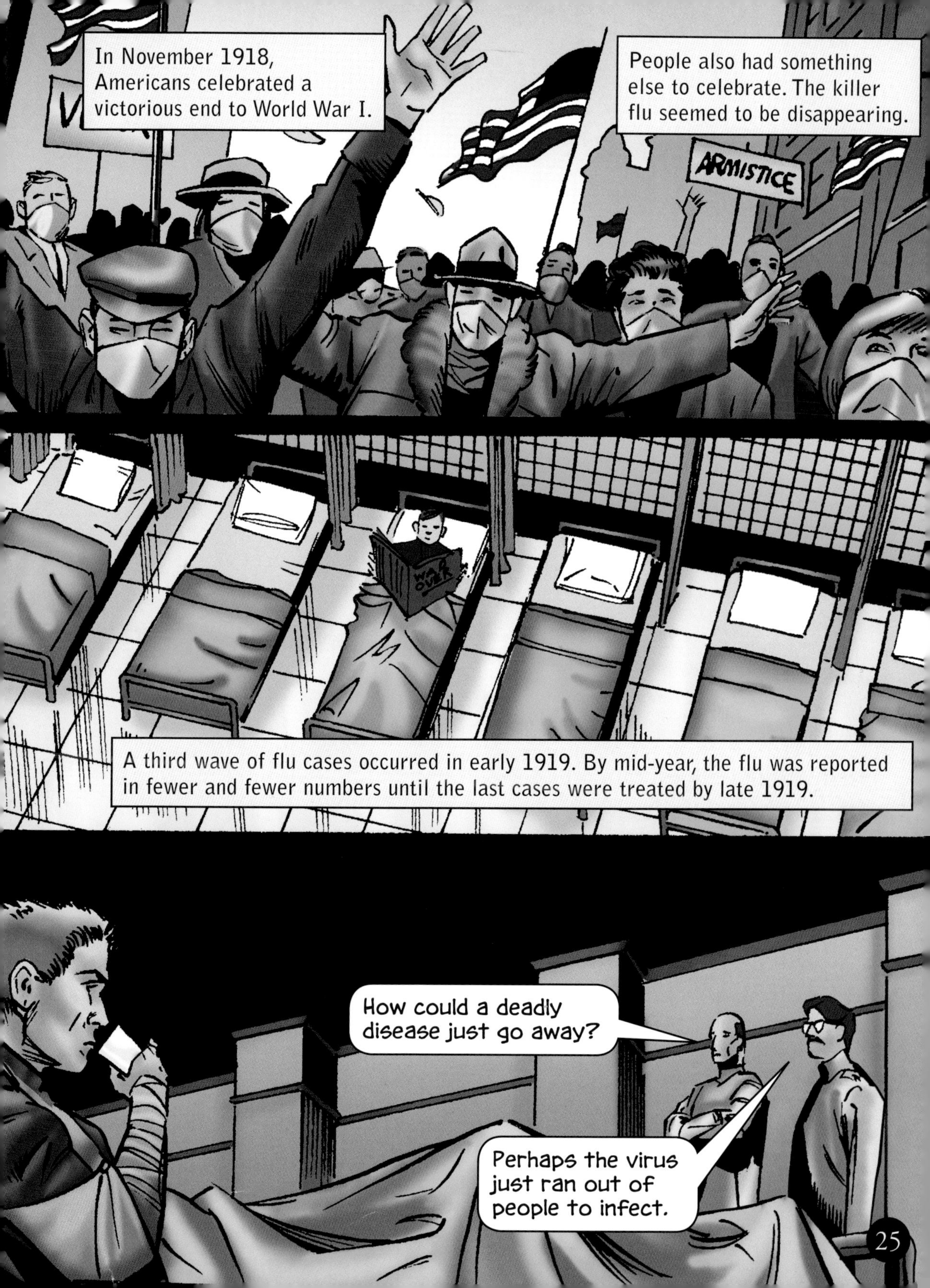
In November 1918, Americans celebrated a victorious end to World War I.
People also had something else to celebrate. The killer flu seemed to be disappearing.
ARMISTICE
A third wave of flu cases occurred in early 1919. By mid-year, the flu was reported in fewer and fewer numbers until the last cases were treated by late 1919.
How could a deadly disease just go away?
Perhaps the virus just ran out of people to infect.

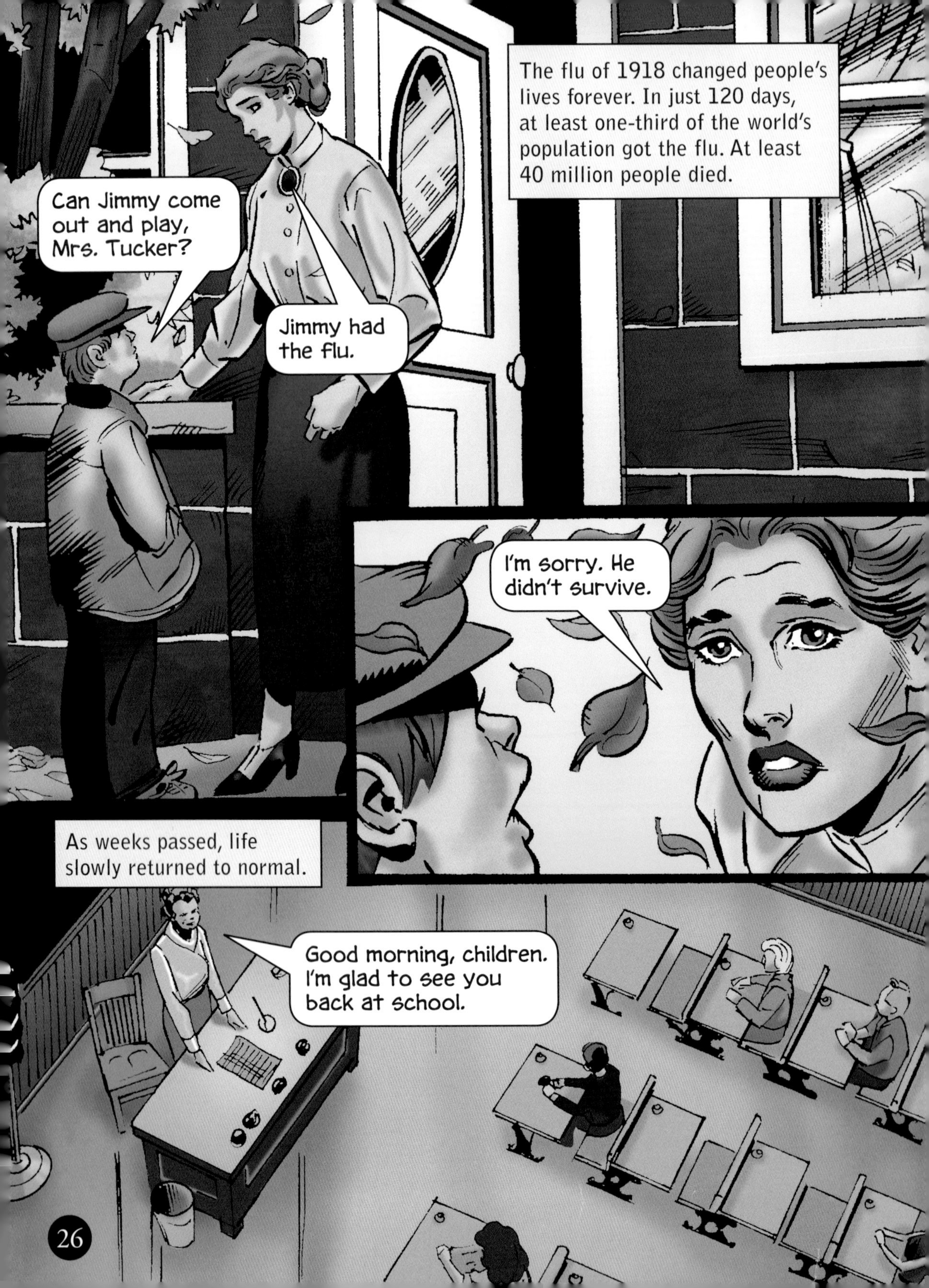
The flu of 1918 changed people's lives forever. In just 120 days, at least one-third of the world's population got the flu. At least 40 million people died.
Can Jimmy come out and play, Mrs. Tucker?
Jimmy had the flu.
I'm sorry. He didn't survive.
As weeks passed, life slowly returned to normal.
Good morning, children. I'm glad to see you back at school.

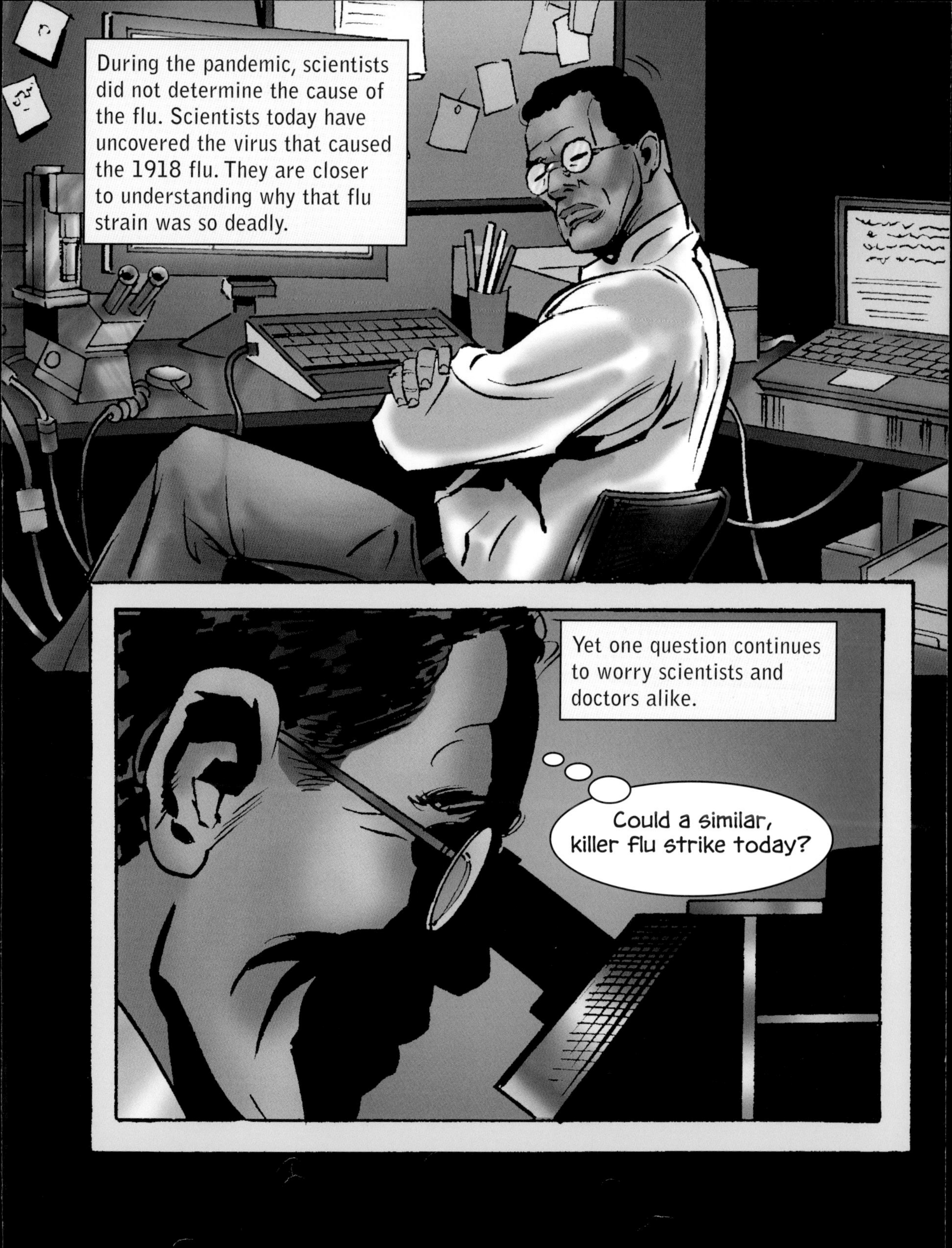
During the pandemic, scientists did not determine the cause of the flu. Scientists today have uncovered the virus that caused the 1918 flu. They are closer to understanding why that flu strain was so deadly.
Yet one question continues to worry scientists and doctors alike.
Could a similar, killer flu strike today?

MORE ABOUT THE 1918 FLU PANDEMIC

- Between 1918 and 1919, influenza killed at least 40 million people worldwide—perhaps more. Some researchers believe the influenza pandemic killed up to 100 million people worldwide. The exact figures are unknown, as reliable records were not kept in all parts of the world at that time.

- Influenza means influence in Italian. In the 1700s, some people thought that the planets, and especially the moon, could influence a person's health and make them sick.

- Spain was hit especially hard by the flu. About 8 million people in Spain suffered from the flu. Because of this outbreak, some people incorrectly believed the virus started in Spain, calling it the Spanish flu.

- About 675,000 Americans died of the flu in 1918. Of those who died from the disease, 43,000 were U.S. soldiers.

- Young children and the elderly are typically most likely to get influenza. However, the 1918 flu was most deadly to people between the ages of 20 and 40.

- The flu of 1918 hit India hard. Fifty out of every 1,000 people in India died from the flu, an estimated 20 million people.

- During the 1918 outbreak, people often died from complications associated with the flu. The lungs of flu victims often filled with fluid, causing them to cough up blood. Their skin often looked blue.

- Not only did the flu pandemic cause a shortage of doctors and nurses, it caused a shortage of undertakers and grave diggers. Many cities ran out of coffins to bury the dead, and flu victims were sometimes buried in large mass graves.

- The 1918 flu vanished as mysteriously as it began. Doctors believe that the virus died out because it ran out of people to infect.

- Today, scientists study lung tissue samples from victims of the 1918 flu pandemic to learn more about the deadly strain. Scientists use this research to learn more about viruses, how they change, and how to fight future outbreaks.

GLOSSARY

camphor (KAM-for)— a gummy, fragrant substance found in the wood and bark of a camphor tree

epidemic (ep-uh-DEM-ik)—an infectious disease that spreads quickly through a community or population group

influenza (in-floo-EN-zuh)—an illness that is like a bad cold with fever and muscle pain; a virus causes influenza.

pandemic (pan-DEM-ik)—a disease that spreads over a wide area and affects many people

quarantine (KWOR-uhn-teen)—limiting or forbidding the movement of people to prevent the spread of disease

stalwart (STAWL-wort)—strength of mind, body, or spirit

strain (STRAYN)—illnesses that share common symptoms but have characteristics that make them different

INTERNET SITES

FactHound offers a safe, fun way to find Internet sites related to this book. All of the sites on FactHound have been researched by our staff.

Here's how:
1. Visit *www.facthound.com*
2. Choose your grade level.
3. Type in this book ID **1429601582** for age-appropriate sites. You may also browse subjects by clicking on letters, or by clicking on pictures and words.
4. Click on the **Fetch It** button.

FactHound will fetch the best sites for you!

READ MORE

Conway, John Richard. *World War I*. U.S. Wars. Berkeley Heights, N.J.: MyReportLinks.com Books, 2003.

Hoffmann, Gretchen. *The Flu*. Health Alert. New York: Marshall Cavendish Benchmark, 2007.

O'Neal, Claire. *The Influenza Pandemic of 1918*. A Robbie Reader. Hockessin, Del.: Mitchell Lane, 2008.

Peters, Stephanie True. *The 1918 Influenza Pandemic*. Epidemic! New York: Benchmark Books, 2005.

BIBLIOGRAPHY

Barry, John M. *The Great Influenza: The Epic Story of the Deadliest Plague in History*. New York: Viking, 2004.

Crosby, Alfred W. *America's Forgotten Pandemic: The Influenza of 1918*. New York: Cambridge University Press, 1989.

Kolata, Gina Bari. *Flu: The Story of the Great Influenza Pandemic of 1918 and the Search for the Virus that Caused It*. New York: Farrar, Straus and Giroux, 1999.

INDEX